Touched by the CHRIST

The followers of Jesus reflect on His final days

Music by Lloyd Larson

Narration by David Burke
Orchestrated by Brant Adams

Editor: Jean Anne Shafferman
Music Engraving: Linda Taylor
Cover Design: Patti Jeffers

ISBN: 978-1-4291-0418-0

Lorenz
www.lorenz.com

Foreword

Perhaps the most distinctive characteristic of Jesus Christ's earthly ministry was the impact He had on the lives of individuals. Though we read about occasions where He ministered to large groups of people, many of the most poignant recordings in the gospels are those moments when Jesus was personally engaged in the life experiences of individuals. Persons who experienced Jesus in this manner were dramatically changed. Some were healed. Others changed their lives and career paths. Some instantly turned from their sinful ways, while others rejected His teachings with hardened hearts. No one, though, left such an encounter with Jesus unchanged in some way.

Touched by the Christ recalls the last days of Jesus' earthly life. It does so, though, through the eyes of individuals who were directly impacted by His ministry. Some of these persons had known Jesus for many years, while others encountered Him for the first time in the final days of His earthly life. Regardless of the context, His influence was significant and life-changing.

The blending of personal narratives and music in this resource is intended to provide a fresh look at the Messiah—the Incarnate God—who came to offer hope for the hurting and broken. *Touched by the Christ* is an invitation to walk the path to the foot of the cross. There we are met by the One who invites us to be changed by His eternal love and grace. It is a reminder that He who changed the lives of individuals in the first century is still in the business of doing so today.

—Lloyd Larson and David Burk

Staging Suggestions

Touched by the Christ is flexibly conceived and can be performed as simply or elaborately as you wish, depending upon your resources and preferences. It may be accompanied by full orchestra or by keyboard alone.

55-60 Minute Special Program

As an inspired 55-60 minute music drama, *Touched by the Christ* can be performed with costumed characters presenting a series of compelling monologues, each paired with a corresponding chorus. Some choruses feature solos, and sets and lighting may be added to enhance the dramatic effect.

10-20 Minute Worship Programs

Directors are encouraged to creatively tailor this flexible resource to provide a variety of 10-20 minute programs that will fit into a standard worship service, depending upon your seasonal needs. For example:

- Palm/Passion Sunday
  Monologue: Mary, sister of Martha/Chorus: *Sing Praise and Hosanna to the King!*
  Monologue: Officer to Caiaphas/Chorus: *The Messiah Has Come!*

- Maundy Thursday
  Monologue: Judas/Chorus: *Lord, Make My Life a Sacrifice*
  Monologue: Peter/Chorus: *Wash My Sinful Spirit*
  Monologue: Jesus/Chorus: *In the Garden He Prayed*

- Good Friday
  Monologue: Pilate/Chorus: *The King of the Jews*
  Monologue: Mary, the mother of Jesus/Chorus: *Ah, Holy Jesus/O Love Divine*

- Easter/Eastertide/Ascension
  Monologue: Mary Magdalene/Chorus: *Glorious, Risen Christ!*
  Monologue: Thomas/Chorus: *By Faith and Not by Sight*

Anthem Drama Resource

Each of the monologue/chorus pairs can be excerpted individually to provide a dramatic 5-6 minute anthem presentation in worship or Sunday school, for special fellowship events, or for community outreach programs.

Staging with One Reader

When one reader is used, the authors recommend that he/she incorporate the suggested props, which are integral to the monologues.

Note: To facilitate performance with one reader only, optional introductions have been added to each monologue. When multiple readers are used, the authors do not recommend the use of the optional introductions.

Staging with Multiple Readers

For performances with multiple characters delivering the monologues, the authors recommend that the characters utilize props, costumes and mannerisms that enable them to dramatically personify their characters.

Cast, Costumes and Props

For performance with staging, you can create "period" costumes and props for each of the following characters:

- **Mary, sister of Martha** – Palm branch

- **Officer to Caiaphas** – Whip of ropes

- **Judas** – Draw-string purse filled with coins

- **Peter** – Crude basin

- **Jesus** – Bible

- **Pilate** – Sign reading "King of the Jews"

- **Mary, the Mother of Jesus** – Small box of herbs

- **Mary Magdalene** – Folded, soiled linen cloth

- **Thomas** – Plate with honeycomb in which one portion is missing

Contents

Companion Products

55/1121L	SAB Score
30/2423L	Orchestral Score and Parts
	2 Fl., Ob., 2 Cl., Bsn., 2 Hn., 3 Tpt., 2 Tbn., Tuba, Timp., Perc., Harp,
	Pno., Vln. 1 & 2, Vla., Cello, Bass
99/2442L	SATB Performance CD
99/2491L	SAB Performance CD
99/2443L	Bulk SATB Performance CDs (10 pak)
99/2492L	Bulk SAB Performance CDs (10 pak)
99/2444L	Accompaniment CD
99/2445L	SA/TB Part-dominant Rehearsal CDs (reproducible)
99/2446L	SA/B Part-dominant Rehearsal CDs (reproducible)
55/1122L	Performance CD/SATB Score Combination
55/1129L	Performance CD/SAB Score Combination

The Cross
(Prelude)

5

Arranged by **Lloyd Larson**
Tunes: ST. CHRISTOPHER by Frederick C. Maker,
HUDSON by Ralph E. Hudson and John H. Hewitt,
and HAMBURG by Lowell Mason

① Solemnly ♩ = ca. 72

10

Optional Introduction:

Join us as we walk with the Christ on His journey to the cross. Listen to the stories of those who met Him along the way. Hear now the story of Mary, sister of Martha.

Monologue: Mary, sister of Martha *(with a palm branch)*

Come with me and draw close to the cross . . . and the Christ of the cross will draw close to you. I know it is true for I came and was touched, touched by the Christ of the cross.

Long before He went to the cross, my heart was drawn to Jesus. At our house in Bethany the face of my Lord was well known. You see, my brother, Lazarus, was dead. And Jesus made him alive! People from all around would come to see the dead man come back to life. Oh, how we loved it when Jesus would stop by the house with His twelve closest friends—the ones who were always with Him . . . in life.

The last time I saw the face of Jesus was as He approached Jerusalem for the greatest week of the year. All Bethany came to our house. Lazarus was even more alive than usual. And Martha, O Martha, my sister, was halfway beside herself. *(shrugs)* She often is. She wanted so badly to please the Lord as He stopped on His way. But somehow I knew—I knew by the look in His eye—that this trip to the Holy City was not like before. And therefore, I anointed Him with my own hand. I poured out all: a vial of precious nard onto His more-precious head. The oil soaked into His full brown hair and the nard ran down to sweeten His one-piece robe.

I drew near to wipe His feet. I did what I could. And He knew my heart as I drew near to His place at the table, for He said, "She's anointed my body beforehand to prepare it for burial." At the time I thought, what a morbid way to receive a sacrificial gift. Some said extravagant. But now I know it was meager, far less than He deserved, for He was the Christ. He *is* the Christ.

My hands would smell of the nard for many days thereafter. In fact, my fingers carried the scent when I cut this palm to wave for Him. "Blessed is the Anointed One! Blessed is He that comes in the name of the Lord!" How precious to know as only I knew that the One on the donkey—the One hailed by crowded masses with palm leaves of worship—still wore the aroma of nard from my vial as He went to the city that day. Oh, how I wish to go back to that day, to that blessed, triumphant day. I wish I could hear the shouts once more of jubilant praise! Fragrant in mind as the smell of nard and aroma of fresh cut palms: "Hosanna! Hosanna! Hosanna to the Christ! Blessed is He that comes in the name of the Lord!"

Sing Praise and Hosanna to the King!

SATB with opt. Unison Choir

Based on
John 12:12-13

Words and Music by
Lloyd Larson

1st time: opt. Unison Choir and/or SA
2nd time: opt. Unison Choir, SA and TB

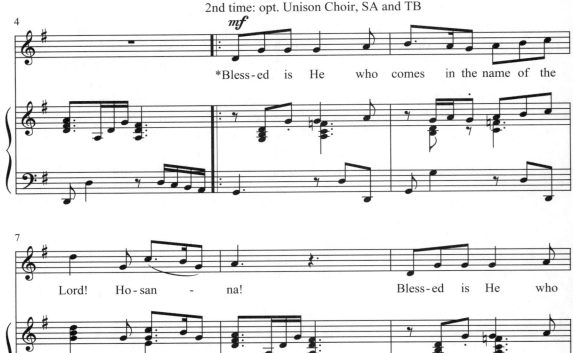

*Bless-ed is He who comes in the name of the Lord! Ho-san - na! Bless-ed is He who

*Measures 4-12 may be repeated as desired to accommodate processional needs. Any number of vocal configurations may be employed to create variety in this section: Unison Choir (if used) alone; Unison Choir and SA voices; Unison Choir, SA and TB voices; and so forth, to list a few.

14

Blessed is He who comes in the name of the Lord! Ho-san - na! He is our long - a - wait - ed King, the Lord strong and might-y; God's on - ly Son, the

- opt. Unis. Choir

16

Optional Introduction:

Jesus encountered both friends and enemies on His journey. Hear now the story of an officer to Caiaphas.

Monologue: Officer to Caiaphas *(with a whip of ropes)*

Don't you dare draw near to that charlatan, to that cursed Man on the cross, to that Man who claimed to be equal with God Himself! We're lucky to finally be rid of Him . . . trouble-maker, rabble-rouser! That's what He was, and that's all that He was—not anything like a Messiah. It's a wonder no lightning fell on His head as He spoke his poison words. "I and my Father are one." Such a Man was too dangerous to live among decent, God-fearing Jews.

And I'm proud to say that I was in on our secret plan from the very first. My Lord, the High Priest Caiaphas, spoke it clear: "Better that one man should die than a whole nation follow a blasphemer and the Romans tighten their grip." So we concocted a master plan to kill Him by any convenient means we could.

Don't look so shocked. We never lifted our hands against Him before He lifted His against us. You see this whip? A tangle of cords, quite painful when slung about in anger. And He was angry the day He used it to drive out honest merchants from the temple. That made my blood boil!

When we finally found His weakest link—a traitor among His twelve close friends—we gave Him a chance to turn from His claims of deity. I heard my Lord Caiaphas ask Him to explain Himself. And He spoke back with insolence! So I drew near to that impudent face and I struck Him a blow with my hand. How did it feel to smack this Man they called the Messiah with my own right hand? It felt right and good.

The Messiah Has Come!

SATB

Words by **J. Paul Williams**
and **Lloyd Larson**

Music by
Lloyd Larson

22

si - ah has come!" The sound is ev - 'ry-where. Pro -

claimed the "King of kings," this man from Gal - i - lee, in

whom God's prom - ise is ful - filled; and

yet there is a chill.

The

crowd in Je - ru - sa - lem crowns Him "King of kings!"

But

24

55/1120L-24

claimed the "King of kings," this man from Gal - i - lee, in

whom God's prom - ise is ful - filled; and

yet there is a chill.

The hearts of the peo - ple, changed by this one Man, are filled with a pas - sion be - cause of what He's done. The

filled with a pas - sion be - cause of what He's done.

whom God's prom - ise is ful - filled; and

yet there is a chill.

Optional Introduction:

Among the friends of Jesus was one who betrayed Him. Hear now the story of His disciple, Judas.

Monologue: Judas *(with a draw-string purse filled with coins)*

Oh, I came near to the Christ of the cross. I came near with my lips but not my heart. I came so close as to offer the kiss of fellowship. And when I did, He looked as if He could not believe it possible. I felt compelled to turn away from His gaze. Though He fascinated me during our years together, I was never deeply touched by His words . . . too philosophical, too other-worldly. I was looking for a Messiah to deliver His people in this world, not in some future world. Self-sacrifice was what He demanded, and that I was never willing to give.

Yet, He trusted me . . . for I was treasurer among our band of twelve. Believe you me, if left to my judgment, things would have been different. No costly sacrifice of expensive nard to wipe anyone's feet. How can you justify that? So many things seem . . . not a sacrifice, but a waste now I think back. The good will of the people sacrificed as He drove out the money changers. The chance to answer the High Priest sacrificed as He spoke defiantly. And yes, the chance to escape to Galilee sacrificed when He went out to the garden to pray, though He knew what I was up to.

He wasted His time with me . . . a total waste. And now that He has been taken to Caiaphas, it's all a waste, a monumental waste with the twelve scattered like sheep. My life and my money are now my own. I drew the cords of the purse so tight that not one coin could escape. Now I will draw another cord so tight that not one wasted breath may escape. His touch on my life was a waste, a pathetic waste. He called His flock to sacrifice. Such sacrifice is always a waste.

Lord, Make My Life a Sacrifice

SATB

Words by **John Parker**
and **Jay Parker**

Music by
Lloyd Larson

reap_____ what they sow.

Lord, make my life a sac - ri - fice un - to You,_____

a ho - ly of-f'ring ac - cept - a - ble and true._____

Broader

Lord, make my life a sac - ri - fice un - to You,

Broader ♩ = ca. 60

a ho - ly of - f'ring ac - cept - a - ble and true.

Teach me to cher - ish and hold each day as new.

40

*Accompaniment CD holds for 5 beats.

55/1120L-40

Optional Introduction:

Another friend was one who would deny Jesus three times. Hear now the story of His disciple, Peter.

Monologue: Peter *(with a crude basin)*

If I stir my hand in this bowl, the waves and ripples will trouble the water. And yet if I remove the hand, the water falls to peace. With these very eyes I saw Him stand in a fishing boat tossed by the thunderous wrath of an angry sea. And with these ears I heard Him say, "Peace, be still." He held up His hand as if to quiet a wailing babe: "Shhhhh. Go to sleep now, child." The waves and the wind obeyed His voice. Our boat stopped careening . . . lay still with puddles sloshing back and forth. He stopped the storm with His word.

Now a deeper storm rages in the sea of my heart . . . wave upon wave. Agony! For I've done the unspeakable! He foretold me I would deny Him. I took Him by the shoulders: "Not I, Lord. I will never deny You." Yet before the cock crowed twice at break of day, His words were fulfilled by the curse in my mouth. As they brought my Lord from trial in Caiaphas's court, bound by a rope to lead Him away to judgment, He searched the crowd for a familiar face. His eyes met mine. I knew. And He knew.

When they took Him to Pilate, I ran. I wept. It was only last night He stirred His hand in this basin. The Master knelt before my place at the table. My mind rebelled, "Why should the Christ kneel down before a sinful man?" And I argued with Him, "No, Lord, you'll never wash my feet."

"If I don't wash your feet," He said, "you have no part with Me."

"Then wash my head and my hands and all of me." He only washed my feet.

O Lord, You were willing to wash me then. How I wish I could go back, go back with You to the upper room. How I long to hear You say, "Yes, Peter, I will wash you. I will make you clean."

Wash My Sinful Spirit

SATB with opt. Male Solo

Words by
David Burke

Music by
Lloyd Larson

44

How can Your love be so true to me when I am so quick to sin? How can You

draw to Your mer - ci - ful side the one who be -

trays You time and a - gain?____ Je - sus, I

bow; wash my sin - ful spir - it now.____

46

55/1120L-46

me, re-store my soul for I long to be washed

in the cleans-ing wat-er of Your grace, Your a-maz-ing

grace. How can Your love be so

48

true to me when I am so quick to

sin?_____ How can You draw to Your

mer - ci - ful side the one who be - trays You

time and a - gain?___ Je - sus, I bow,

wash my sin - ful spir - it___

hum - bly I bow;

now.___

*Accompaniment CD holds for 6 beats.

Optional Introduction:

The journey to the cross was fraught with struggle. Hear now the words of Jesus.

Monologue: Jesus *(with a Bible in hand)*

Come to Me, all you who are weary and heavily burdened, and I will give you rest. Come to Me . . . come to Me.

My soul is overcome with grief to the point of death. Stay here for a while and watch with Me.

O My Father, if it be possible, let this cup be taken from Me. Yet not as I will, but let Your will be done.

Father, the time has come. Glorify Your Son, that Your Son may glorify You. For You granted Me authority over all people that I might give eternal life to all those You have given Me. Now this is eternal life: that they may know You, the only true God, and Jesus Christ, whom You have sent.

I have brought You glory on earth by completing the work You gave me to do. And now, Father, glorify Me in Your presence with the glory I had with You before the world began.

I have manifested Your name to the men You have given Me out of the world. I am coming to You now, but I say these things while I am still in the world, so that they may have the full measure of My joy within them. I have given them Your word. The world has hated them, for they are not of the world any more than I am of the world.

My prayer is not that You take them out of the world, but that You protect them from the Evil One. My prayer is not for them alone. I pray also for those *(music begins)* who will believe in Me through their message.

Come to Me, all you who are weary and heavily burdened, and I will give you rest. Come to Me . . . . come to Me.

In the Garden He Prayed

SATB

Words by **Lloyd Larson**
Based on Mark 14:32-50

Music by
Lloyd Larson

52

to the ground where He prayed,____

"Fa - ther, O ho - ly Fa - ther, my

cresc.

soul is dark and dis - mayed.____

cresc.

54

there in the gar - den He prayed.

26 *mp*

Sol - diers with clubs came to

seize Him as there in the gar - den He

prayed. Je-sus, the cho-sen One of God, Son of the great I AM, sent to re-deem the

58

world in love, Je - sus, God's ho - ly

Lamb! It was

there in the gar - den He prayed.

*Accompaniment CD holds for 6 beats.

Optional Introduction:

The Roman Prefect struggled to condemn Jesus to death. Hear now the words of Pontius Pilate.

Monologue: Pilate *(with a sign reading "King of the Jews")*

Too much has been spoken of the Nazarene. Yet much remains untold. Puzzling, yes? He drew the attention of many: from the lowest right up to myself. He even drew the attention of my wife. Yes, Pilate's wife dreamed of the Christ. I have sentenced hundreds of men to hang on a cross, but only this One troubled the dreams of my household. She said, "Have nothing to do with the blood of this just Man." She was convinced, as though she'd seen the truth. But a man cannot govern by the dreams of his wife!

I have spies in all quarters, and I knew the people called Him their chosen, anointed King, their Messiah. So I put the question to Him straight up as He stood there. "Are You the King of the Jews?" I looked at His bound hands.

"You have said it right." He spoke in a humble voice, "For this reason I was born, and for this cause I came into the world, to bear witness to the truth. For everyone who seeks the truth hears My voice."

(laughs) That really said it all. The Man spoke as though He actually was the truth! I know a bit about truth, and for one Man to say that everyone who seeks it follows Him . . . well, that's a bit too much for me to swallow. "What is truth?" I asked. I could have elaborated. Your truth? My truth? The truth of those whose voices are screaming outside my window? There are many competing truths!

Yet still I knew He did not deserve to die. I reached out my hand and touched His shoulder to lead Him onto the balcony. "I find no fault in Him."

Thousands of angry voices rang through the Praetorium: "Crucify Him! Crucify Him!"

"Would you rather I release this man or Barabbas, the criminal?"

"Not this man, but Barabbas." Then I did the worst I could to set Him free. I had Him scourged to arouse their pity, allowed Him to be dressed in a purple robe and crowned with thorns so they would soften. But they would not hear of it. My only revenge is this sign which I dictated for His cross: not "He claimed to be King of the Jews" as they pleaded it might be, but as He had spoken it. I wrote the truth: "King of the Jews."

The King of the Jews

SATB

Words and Music by
Lloyd Larson

www.lorenz.com
LT

64

are the ones who sang His praise: "He is our King!," their ho-

san - nas raised. "The lone - ly path is His to walk." His

"The lone - ly path is His to walk."

fol-l'wers mourn, the scorn-ers mock.

Christ

Optional Introduction:

Imagine the struggle of Mary, the mother of Jesus. Hear now her words.

Monologue: Mary, the Mother of Jesus *(with a small box of herbs)*

Words? I have no words for what I saw today. The world itself cannot contain the words that should be spoken. Can a mother recount in words the death of her child? Can a child of God recount in words the death of God? Yet I must find words.

I watched as He dragged a wooden cross through the street. Hands that knew only kindness . . . I saw torn by nails! Feet that knew only righteousness . . . torturously pinned to the wood! And I witnessed His heart, His pure heart . . . pierced by their hate! Three hours He hung between heaven and earth on a cross.

I remember the day when my Boy ran to me with the tiniest splinter. It stings the heart of a mother to see the suffering of her child. So it is, for this day, for this scene on the hill . . . I have no words. Other words I must find from former days.

Words of the angel yet ring in my ears: "Of His kingdom there shall be no end." No end! That's what the angel Gabriel said to me. No end! If a cross is not an end, then what is it?

Words of warning from aged Simeon at the temple when we took Jesus for dedication. He said to me, "A sword shall pierce your soul." How could Simeon know? And yet his words comfort me now as only truth can comfort.

Words of my Jesus Himself echo in the ear of His mother. I can still hear the first words His lips ever spoke. And I have heard the last. He raised a cry with loud voice: "It is finished!" His breath did not return. But the angel said: "Of His kingdom there shall be no end." How can these words stand side by side? "It is finished!" "There shall be no end."

This box in my hand I have held in keeping 33 years. Jesus saw it in our home all through His life. *(music begins)* It was given Him by a wise man from the East as I held my tiny Baby in my arms, His little fingers reaching to my face, His tiny toenails wrapped in ragged cloth. It is myrrh, embalming spice. "What a gift to give a babe," I always thought. And yet, at the cross, it was a comfort to me. Little Jesus touched my face so often as a Child. Today, with myrrh, I touched the face of my Boy to anoint Him for the shroud.

Ah, Holy Jesus/O Love Divine

SATB

Words by **Johann Heermann**;
trans. **Robert Bridges**, *alt.*
and **Charles Wesley**, *alt.*

Arranged by **Lloyd Larson**
Quoting PASSION CHORALE by **Hans Leo Hassler**
and HERZLIEBSTER JESU by **Johann Crüger**

70

55/1120L-70

74

*Accompaniment CD holds for 5 beats.

/1120L-74

Optional Introduction:

Picture the dawn of victory! Hear now the words of Mary Magdalene on the first day of the new week.

Monologue: Mary Magdalene *(with a folded, soiled linen cloth)*

I came near to the cross as the body of my Lord hung motionless between heaven and earth. His lungs no longer gasped for a torturous gulp of air. His limbs were stiff as I helped to wrap the lifeless body in winding cloth. His skin was cold and bloodless and pale. There was no doubt that Jesus was dead. But that was Friday.

And today was the first day of the new week. If someone else had told me, I'd never have believed it. But the tomb was empty and this . . . this was left behind—the linen cloth with which His head was wrapped. All was confusion, and I wept that someone had taken His corpse. A man stood near; the gardener, I assumed. "Where have you taken Him? Where was He put?" Then He spoke my name, and I saw. He was there!

I fell at His feet to hold on and keep Him from leaving again. And His skin . . . His skin was not as I felt it on Friday! It was changed. No longer cold and stiff and pale. It was . . . it was impossible to describe what His skin was like, but finer than the flesh of any baby that had ever been born. Alive . . . yes! But more than alive. His skin seemed to glow with new life—vibrant life, a life beyond all human knowledge. Eternal life flowing through the eternal Christ as He stood before me in resurrected power.

Then I noticed them—the wounds. Not bloody or deformed. Transformed from scars of flesh and blood into miraculous, beautiful, perfect signs of His glorious power over death. He stood before me, more alive than anyone I've ever seen. He who was dead is now alive. He said not to hold Him for He must ascend to His Father and to my Father. But I do hold Him. I hold Him still, dear in the depth of my heart.

Glorious, Risen Christ!

SATB

Words by
David Burke

Music by
Lloyd Larson

emp - ty room; the Son of God was gone!

cresc.

SA

Glo - rious, ris - en Christ! A-

TB

live and robed in maj - es - ty!

Yet the scars of the cross show the

78

55/1120L-78

maj - es - ty! Yet the scars of the cross show the in - fi - nite cost, the mi -

Yet the cross shows the in - fi - nite cost,

rac - u - lous touch the life-chang-ing touch of Christ's

God's ho - ly touch,

love for me!

84

Optional Introduction:

Envision doubt transformed to steadfast faith! Hear now the words of Thomas, the believer.

Monologue: Thomas *(with a honeycomb on a plate, one portion missing)*

How many of you have ever taken a bite from a honeycomb . . . such as this? So have I. Most of us enjoy the chewy chunk of waxy sweetness. But when they told me that my Lord and Master who was dead and buried . . . that *He* had taken a bite from this very honeycomb, I was . . . well, I think, understandably skeptical. Would you have believed were you in my place? The others were excited . . . ecstatic. I knew something had happened. Perhaps a vision, or a stranger mistaken at a distance. But to actually insist that the Son of God Himself had stood in their very presence—solid flesh and bone—to join them for a bite of whitefish and honeycomb? Preposterous! You would have said the same. I only stated the obvious: "Unless I can put my hand where the spear went in and insert my finger into the holes made by the nails . . . unless I touch Him for myself, I'll never believe!" You would have said the same. Admit it.

But one week later, when He stood before me and reached out those very hands . . . I didn't need to touch. I bowed and said, "My Lord and my God!" You would have said the same. Then Jesus said the sweetest words, sweeter to *your* ears, I imagine, than even honey from a honeycomb. He said, "Thomas, because you have seen, you've believed. Blessed are the ones who have not seen and yet have believed." He spoke that day of you, my brother, my sister, if you believe on the Christ. And for your simple faith, He promises a blessing, a blessing that even His closest disciples never knew. This is the sweet gift He offers to each of you. If you will by faith draw near to Him—draw near to the Christ of the cross—He will draw near to you. And as He has promised, Jesus will touch your life. He will change your life. And this Jesus, the Christ, will come to dwell in you, and you in Him, forevermore. Amen.

By Faith and Not by Sight

SATB

Words by **Henry Alford**,
Lloyd Larson and **Ray Palmer**

Music by **Lloyd Larson**
Quoting OLIVET by **Lowell Mason**

88

55/1120L-88

near, and seek where You are found; that, when our

near,

life of faith is done, in realms of clear - er

light, we may be - hold You as You are, with full and

92

*Accompaniment CD holds for 5 beats.